Made in the USA
Columbia, SC
01 May 2024

35146449R00028